Tyrannosaurus Rex

and other Cretaceous Meat-Eaters
8202320

by Daniel Cohen

Capstone Press
MINNEAPOLIS

Printed in the United States of America.

Capstone Press • 2440 Fernbrook Lane • Minneapolis, MN 55447

Editorial Director	John Coughlan
Managing Editor	Tom Streissguth
Production Editor	James Stapleton
Book Design	Timothy Halldin

Library of Congress Cataloging-in-Publication Data

Cohen, Daniel, 1936-
    Tyrannosaurus rex and other Cretaceous meat-eaters / Daniel Cohen.
      p. cm. -- (Dinosaurs of North America)
    Includes bibliographical references (p. 42) and index.
    Summary: Describes the dinosaurs of the period from 140 to 65 million years ago when the earth underwent dramatic changes.
    ISBN 1-56065-288-8
    1. Tyrannosaurus rex--Juvenile literature. 2. Deinonychus--Juvenile literature. 3. Stenonychosaurus - -Juvenile literature. [1. Tyrannosaurus rex. 2. Deinonychus. 3. Stenonychosaurus. 4. Dinosaurs.] I. Title. II. Series: Cohen, Daniel, 1936- Dinosaurs of North America.
    QE862.S3C57   1996
    567.9'7--dc20   95-11257
                                                               CIP
                                                               AC

Table of Contents

Chapter 1
When They Lived

Terrifying killing machines. Huge lumbering beasts. Small, swift flesh eaters.

Dinosaurs. They came in all shapes and sizes. They roamed the earth for millions of years. And the **Cretaceous** (cret-AY-shus) period marks their end, the final era of the Age of Dinosaurs.

Dinosaurs first appeared on the earth more than 200 million years ago. It was during the

To its prey, the sight of an attacking Tyrannosaurus rex must have been a terrifying sight.

5

Dinosaur bones were found at this site near Drumheller, Alberta.

age that scientists call the **Triassic** (try-ASS-ic) period. **Mammals** appeared at about the same time. But while the mammals remained small and unimportant, the dinosaurs flourished.

The Jurassic World

The next period, the **Jurassic** (joo-RASS-ic), lasted from 195 million to 140 million years ago. Dinosaurs dominated the land

masses of the earth. The Jurassic period was an age of giants. Some dinosaurs of the period were the largest land animals the world has ever known.

At one time, most of the land masses on earth were clumped together in a single supercontinent. By the Jurassic period, the supercontinent began to break apart. But it was still possible for dinosaurs to move with ease from one part of the world to another.

Prehistoric Weather

Earth's climate during the Jurassic period was warmer and wetter than it is today. It was also more uniform. There were no polar ice caps and no severe storms. During the Jurassic period the earth was flatter and there were no major mountain ranges.

The plants of the Jurassic world did not look like the plants of the modern world. They were mostly ferns, mosses, and **conifers** (cone-bearing trees). Some of these plants grew to enormous size and provided food for the giant dinosaurs.

Quaternary Age
1.8m to present
65m   Tertiary Age   1.8m
140m Cretaceous Age 65m
195m   Jurassic Age   140m
230m   Triassic Age   195m
280m   Permian Age   230m
345m Carboniferous 280m
395m Devonian Age 345m
435m   Silurian Age   395m
500m Ordovcian Age 435m
700m Cambrian Age 500m

Birds
Mammals

Reptiles
Amphibians

Fish
Primitive chordate

During the Cretaceous period 140 million to 65 million years ago, the earth underwent dramatic changes. The continents drifted farther apart. The world began to look a lot more like it does today. There was tremendous volcanic and other geological activity. Great mountain ranges rose and new islands were formed. In the Cretaceous era, dinosaurs could no longer move easily from one part of the world to another.

The earth's climate also changed. It became colder in places and the temperature ranges became more extreme. As a result of all these changes, new types of plants first appeared during the Cretaceous period. There were the familiar flowering plants and trees that we know today. Plant-eating dinosaurs of the middle and late Cretaceous fed on magnolia, laurel, dogwood, rose, grape vine, oak, poplar, willow, birch, and others.

Dinosaurs walked the earth during the Triassic, Jurassic, and Cretaceous periods, at the same time that mammals and birds first appeared.

9

The mammals remained small. Many resembled the modern shrew and opossum. There were new types of amphibians, such as frogs. Among the reptiles there were many new species of turtles and tortoises and, for the first time, snakes.

Extinction and Evolution

The largest of the dinosaurs, the great **sauropods**, could not survive the worldwide changes. Like many other dinosaur species, they became extinct during the Cretaceous period. But overall, the dinosaurs as a group continued to flourish. Many new dinosaur species evolved to replace those that had disappeared.

Huge herds of **ceratopsian**, or horn-faced, dinosaurs roamed the western parts of what is now North America. They grazed on the new varieties of plants. The **hadrosaurs**, or duck-billed, dinosaurs did not evolve until the middle of the Cretaceous period. But soon an astonishing variety of these creatures inhabited most of the world. Their teeth adapted to

The skull of a plant-eating hadrosaur.

chewing the tougher plants that now grew so widely.

But it was among the **carnivorous**, or meat-eating, dinosaurs that the most spectacular of the creatures appeared. The Cretaceous period was the time of Tyrannosaurus, the largest and most fearsome predator that ever lived. And among the small predators were those that do not fit the image of dinosaurs as slow and stupid creatures.

A Mysterious End

So, despite the changes that took place during the Cretaceous period, the dinosaurs seem to have adapted to them very well. And then, 65 million years ago, at the end of the Cretaceous period, all the dinosaurs were gone.

A few species may have survived the end of the Cretaceous period for a brief time. But even that is uncertain. What we do know is that the dinosaurs, which had ruled the earth for 150 million years, disappeared.

Extinction is part of life on earth. The vast majority of all the species that have ever existed are now extinct. During the 150 million years in which the dinosaurs were dominant, many species became extinct. But new species of dinosaurs evolved to take their place. The sudden and complete disappearance of such a large and successful group as the dinosaurs is difficult to explain.

At one time, scientists believed that the dinosaurs simply failed to adapt to the many other changes of the Cretaceous period. But

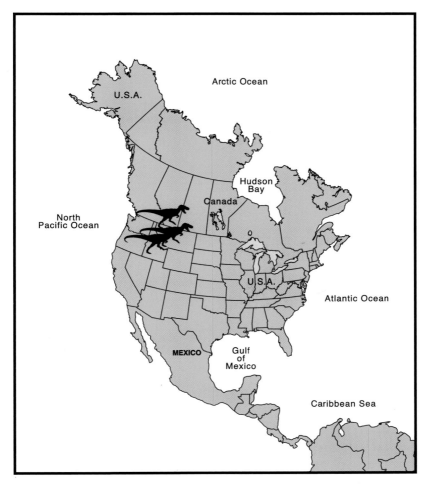

Tyrannosaurus bones have been discovered in the western United States and Canada.

dinosaurs had already adapted to many changes. And the dinosaurs were not the only creatures to die out at the end of the Cretaceous period. Great marine reptiles, flying reptiles, and many smaller animals also disappeared.

Now the most popular theory is that there was some sort of worldwide catastrophe 65 million years ago. Perhaps the earth was struck by a **comet** or an **asteroid**. Such an impact would have triggered a chain of rapid worldwide changes. But not all scientists agree. The disappearance of the dinosaurs remains one of the great scientific mysteries.

All we can say for sure is that the great tribe of dinosaurs, the largest and in many ways the most magnificent land animals in the history of the earth, disappeared. That left the earth open for our ancestors, the mammals.

Tyrannosaurus was the most fearsome predator of the Cretaceous period.

Tyrannosaurus Rex

(Ty-RAN-oh-SAW-rus)
tyrant reptile
Range: *Western United States and Canada*
Length: *40 feet (12 meters)*
Weight: *8 tons (7.2 metric tons)*

Tyrannosaurus, or the largest known species, Tyrannosaurus rex (king tyrant reptile), is probably the best known of all the dinosaurs. Not very many Tyrannosaurus **fossils** have actually been found, although a nearly complete skeleton was unearthed in 1990 in South Dakota. But reproductions and models can be seen in almost all museum dinosaur collections. It is hard to imagine a dinosaur film being made without Tyrannosaurus putting in an appearance.

Tyrannosaurus was not the largest dinosaur that ever existed. But it was the largest meat-eating dinosaur. It was also probably the most terrifying predator that ever existed. From the time that the first Tyrannosaurus fossils were unearthed and recognized in the early years of the 20th century, the creature has fascinated us.

The most impressive feature of Tyrannosaurus is its massive skull. The skull is much heavier and stronger than that of similar carnivorous dinosaurs like Allosaurus. The huge mouth is filled with sharp, saberlike teeth, some seven inches (18 centimeters) long. The massive head is supported by a short and powerful neck.

The terrifying Tyrannosaurus was actually slow on its feet. Scientists believe it may have been a lurking predator—one that lies in wait for its prey.

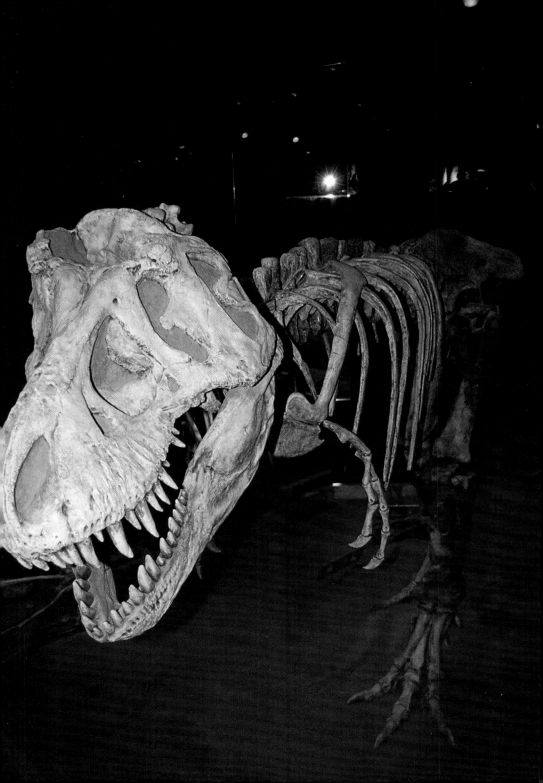

The creature's body is thick. Its hind legs are huge and powerful. Its toes end in sharply curved **talons**. A long tail was used to balance the heavy front end of Tyrannosaurus.

Small, Strange Limbs

The arms and hands of Tyrannosaurus are among its most bizarre features. Most dinosaurs of this type have small forelegs or arms. But in Tyrannosaurus this trend seems to have been taken to an extreme. Its arms are tiny compared with the overall size of the animal. And they end in useless looking, small hands with only two claws. Tyrannosaurus looks oddly unbalanced.

As with most dinosaurs, there has been some controversy over how Tyrannosaurus lived. At one time, many scientists believed that the creature was a slow-moving **scavenger**. It seemed too heavy to be able to actively run down prey. It would have to feed on the remains of already dead creatures that could not run away or fight back effectively.

Tyrannosaurus had a huge skull and very short arms.

How They Hunted

The longer scientists examined the evidence, the more they came to feel that Tyrannosaurus was an active predator. The long, strong legs of this dinosaur would have allowed it to cover a lot of ground very quickly. Its bulk, however,

made it hard for Tyrannosaurus to pursue its prey for very long.

A popular theory today is that Tyrannosaurus was a lurking predator. It would wait in hiding for prey to pass, then catch it after a short chase. It would leap out at a victim in a short burst of speed. Charging with mouth open wide, it could hit its victim at 20 miles (32 kilometers) per hour. The force of the impact would be absorbed by Tyrannosaurus's sturdy skull and powerful neck.

The main prey of Tyrannosaurus were probably hadrosaurs, the duck-billed dinosaurs that traveled in large herds. The shock of being hit by a charging Tyrannosaurus would almost certainly have stunned any hadrosaur. Once subdued, the victim would be rapidly sliced open by the large sharp teeth of the predator. Violent twisting and tugging of the head, aided

The teeth of Tyrannosaurus were several inches long and razor-sharp.

by the powerful neck muscles, would have torn apart the most powerful **sinews**. Great chunks of flesh and bone could have been bitten off and swallowed whole.

The charge of a Tyrannosaurus must have been one of the most frightening spectacles in the entire history of life on earth.

Deinonychus

(DY-noh-NIKE-us)
terrible claw
Range: *Western United States*
Length: *13 feet (3.9 meters)*
Weight: *150 pounds (67.5 kilograms)*

In 1964, a team of **paleontologists**, scientists who study life in past ages, discovered hundreds of bones of an entirely new type of dinosaur in southern Montana. The discoverers gave the small carnivorous

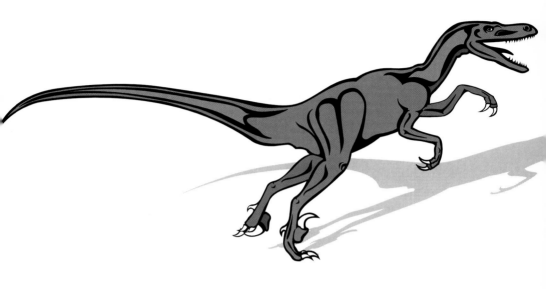

Deinonychus used its long claws to attack its victims.

dinosaur the name Deinonychus, which means terrible claw. The most remarkable feature of this new dinosaur was the second toe on each foot. It ended in a large sickle-shaped claw.

Deinonychus was a lightly built dinosaur that stood about 6 feet (1.8 meters) tall. It had a large head and large mouth. The many teeth, which curved backward, were serrated, with

sharp irregular edges. The teeth allowed the dinosaur to tear great chunks of flesh from its victims.

Grasping Arms

The arms were fairly long for a dinosaur of this type. The hands had three fingers each, ending in long, curved claws. Unlike Tyrannosaurus, where the tiny arms appear nearly useless, the arms of Deinonychus could have been used for grasping.

Bones in the tail show that it was held out stiffly behind the animal. The tail would have been a good counterweight for the dinosaur when it was running. The tail was flexible enough to swing from side to side. This would have helped the dinosaur change direction even when running at full speed.

The legs of Deinonychus were long and thin, with four clawed toes on each foot. It was

Many Deinonychus bones have been discovered in Canada and the United States, especially in Montana.

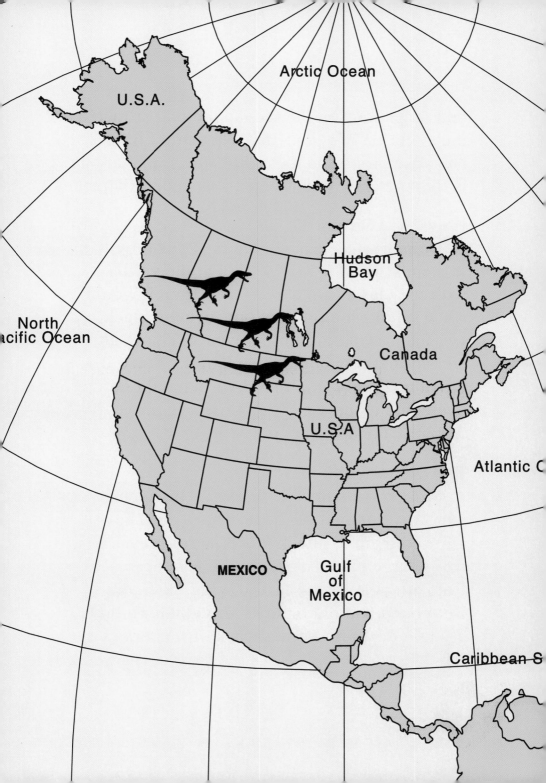

Arctic Ocean

U.S.A.

North
acific Ocean

Hudson
Bay

Canada

U.S.A

Atlantic C

MEXICO

Gulf
of
Mexico

Caribbean S

that large claw on the second toe that attracted the attention of scientists. What could it have been used for? The most probable explanation is that the claw was used as a weapon of attack.

How They Hunted

Deinonychus probably grasped its prey with its hands. Then it would slash at the victim with the claws of its hind feet. Often it would stand on one leg to carry out such an attack.

This method of hunting would require an animal that was both fast and agile. Since it was a relatively small predator, it could not overcome its prey by brute force. It was certainly no slow-moving scavenger.

The Deinonychus Pack

Most scientists believe that Deinonychus must have hunted in packs. This would have allowed them to attack much larger prey. The really large plant eaters would have been safe from attack by these fast-moving predators. But young and old or sick individuals could be brought down by a small pack of hunters in the

same way that a moose or elk is hunted by a pack of wolves. Medium-sized or smaller plant eaters would have been easier prey.

The 1964 Montana find of Deinonychus fossils did more than any other single discovery of modern times to change our attitude toward dinosaurs. When dinosaurs were first discovered, most people still thought of them as stupid, slow-moving giants that became extinct because they were too big to survive. That is what we still mean today when we call something a dinosaur.

But here was a dinosaur that quite obviously was not slow moving or stupid. It wasn't even very large. And its big skull indicates it had a good brain. There is a great deal that we still do not know about Deinonychus and other dinosaurs. But we do know that they were not all stupid and slow-moving giants.

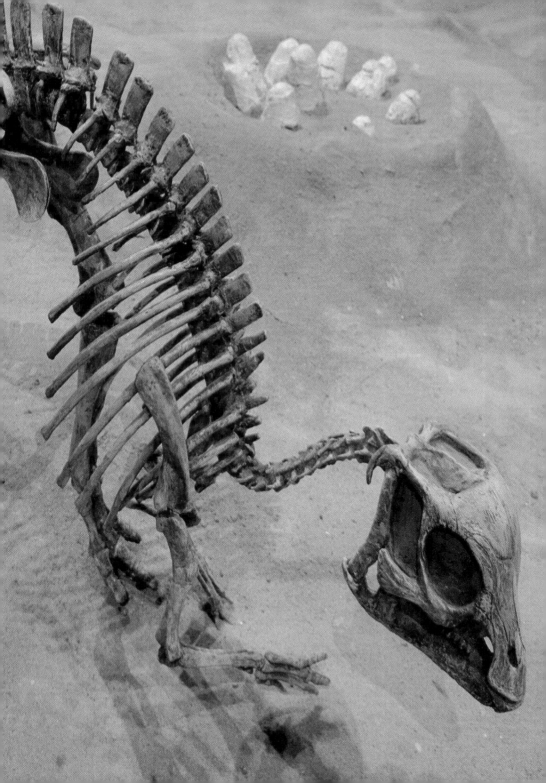

Stenonychosaurus

(STEN-on-NIKE-oh-SAW-rus)
slender-clawed reptile
Range: *Western United States and Canada*
Length: *6 feet (1.8 meters)*
Weight: *50 pounds (22.5 meters)*

Stenonychosaurus, a small meat-eating dinosaur, may have been the brainiest dinosaur that ever lived. The brain cavity relative to body size is the largest of any dinosaur discovered so far.

Most of the time when dinosaurs are discussed, the emphasis is on how small their brains were. The famous dinosaur Stegosaurus, for example, weighed two tons (1.8 metric

Stenonychosaurus was smaller, but more intelligent, than many dinosaurs.

tons) and had a brain the size of a walnut. This led people to believe that dinosaurs were very stupid.

Stenonychosaurus was about the size of an emu, a large flightless bird that lives today. But the dinosaur had a bigger brain. Scientists think that it was about as smart as an opossum. That does not make it particularly brainy by modern standards. But it was not a brainless mountain of flesh either. Stenonychosaurus is another creature that helped change the traditional view of dinosaurs.

Dinosaur Brains

Most of the brain capacity was not concerned with reasoning or other activities that we call intelligence. The brain was used for the creature's highly developed senses, control of its limbs, and quick reflexes.

This dinosaur was a lightly built and active hunter of such small prey as lizards and small mammals. It did not seem to have such weapons as large teeth or claws to go after big

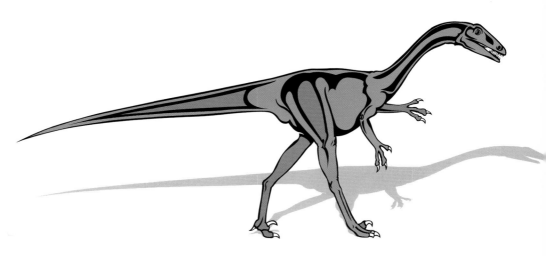

The Stenonychosaurus is also known as Troödon.

prey like other dinosaurs. Instead, Stenonychosaurus had long arms and clawed hands that would have been used to catch and hold small prey.

Its eyes were unusually large and pointed forward. This probably meant that the dinosaurs had overlapping vision that allowed them to see in three dimensions. This would

have been a tremendous advantage for hunters of small swift prey. They may have been active at dusk, or even at night, when mammals were more likely to move around.

The Evolution of Stenonychosaurus

In 1982 scientists published an article speculating about what dinosaurs might have evolved into if they had not become extinct at the end of the Cretaceous period. As their model they used Stenonychosaurus. They suggested that it might have become a highly intelligent creature with hands that were very nearly as good at manipulating objects as a human hand. It would have developed a larger brain and a short neck. It would have walked fully upright and not needed its balancing tail.

This theoretical creature, which the scientists labeled a "dinosauroid," would not have been as swift as Stenonychosaurus. But what it lacked in speed it would have more than made up for with intelligence. It would have been able to avoid potential enemies by outwitting them rather than simply outrunning

them. As a predator, it would have been able to catch prey by running or by ambush. It may also have been able to make and use simple weapons.

All of this, of course, is sheer speculation. There is really no way of predicting what path evolution might have taken if the dinosaurs had not died out. But it is the sort of speculation that makes you think. Certainly 20 or 30 years ago few scientists would have speculated about the possibility of intelligent dinosaurs.

Chapter 3

How Dinosaurs are Discovered

We know that dinosaurs roamed the earth millions of years ago. Yet their remains continue to be discovered by scientists even now. How is it possible that dinosaur bones can be preserved for so many years? The answer lies in the process of fossilization.

When a dinosaur died, several different things could happen to its body. Animals may have eaten its flesh. Smaller animals and even bacteria could have eaten and removed the soft tissue of the dinosaur. Many times, the

dinosaur bones could have been crushed or broken as the flesh was removed from the skeleton. So it is possible that many dinosaur bones simply disintegrated before they could be preserved by nature.

Turning into Rock

However, many dinosaur remains in desert climates were covered with windblown sand before they could be eaten or decompose. Others were washed into lakes or rivers and covered with mud. As the years went by, more and more sand and mud covered these dinosaurs. Over time, this sand and mud turned into rock. Over the course of thousands of years, chemicals in the rocks seeped into the dinosaur remains and turned them into rock, too. The hardened dinosaur remains are then called fossils.

Footprints made by dinosaurs have also been preserved by becoming fossils. So have dinosaur eggs, nests, and dung. All dinosaur fossils provide scientists with valuable

Paleontologists use many different tools to carefully dig dinosaur bones from the ground.

information about these incredible animals and their life on earth.

Buried in Rock

Dinosaur fossils have been found on every continent on earth. In most cases, they are buried in rock. Scientists attempt to unearth the fossils carefully with as little damage as possible to the remains.

The first step in excavating, or removing the fossils from the earth, is to take away the

surrounding soil and rock. Large diggers and bulldozers do this work until the fossils are close to the surface. Then scientists work with small hand tools like hammers and chisels to remove the remaining rock.

Careful Record-Keeping

Once the fossils are exposed, the scientists take great care to record everything they find. Bones are measured and photographed. Extensive notes and diagrams record exactly how the skeleton parts are connected.

As the bones are removed from the digging site, they are numbered and recorded. Then they are carefully packed into padded crates. If a bone is weak or crumbly, it is not removed until it is sprayed with a special hard-setting foam. Sometimes, plaster-soaked bandages are used to harden the bone.

Once all the fossils have been recorded from a site, they are carefully shipped to the scientists' laboratories. There the bones are rebuilt to show how the dinosaur looked while it was living and the dinosaurs ruled the earth.

Glossary

asteroid–small planets or fragments of planets in our solar system

carnivorous–describes a species that can eat and digest meat

Ceratopsian–a horn-faced dinosaur

comet–celestial bodies made up of frozen gas and pieces of rock that pass through the solar system

conifers–cone-bearing trees

Cretaceous period–the third geological period in the Age of Dinosaurs, from 140 million to 65 million years ago

extinction–the death of a group of plants or animals

fossils–the remains of something that once lived

hadrosaurs–plant-eating dinosaurs with broad, flat snouts

herbivorous–describes an animal that can eat and digest plants and vegetation

Jurassic period–the second geological period in the Age of Dinosaurs, from 195 million to 140 million years ago

mammal–an animal with hair and that feeds its young with milk. Examples of mammals include mice, rabbits, dogs, and humans.

paleontologists–scientists who study life in past ages

sauropod–a large, four-legged, plant-eating dinosaur.

scavenger–an animal that feeds upon dead or decayed matter.

sinews–cords of tough tissue attaching the muscles to the bones

talons–sharp claws

Triassic period–the first geological period in the Age of Dinosaurs, from 230 million to 195 million years ago

To Learn More

Arnold, Caroline. *Dinosaur Mountain: Graveyard of the Past*. New York: Clarion Books, 1989.

Benton, Michael. *The Dinosaur Encyclopedia*. New York: Julian Messner, 1984.

Berenstain, Michael. *King of the Dinosaurs, Tyrannosaurus Rex*. Racine, Wis.: Golden, 1989.

Cohen, Daniel and Cohen, Susan. *Where to Find Dinosaurs Today*. New York: Cobblehill, 1992.

Horner, John R. and Lessem, Don. *Digging Up Tyrannosaurus*. New York: Crown, 1992.

Lasky, Kathryn. *Dinosaur Dig*. New York: Morrow Junior Books, 1990.

Lauber, Patricia. *Dinosaurs Walked Here and Other Stories Fossils Tell*. New York: Bradbury Press, 1991.

Lindsay, William. *The Great Dinosaur Atlas.* New York: Julian Messner, 1991.

Murphy, Jim. *The Last Dinosaur.* New York: Scholastic, 1988.

Sandell, Elizabeth J. *Tyrannosaurus Rex: The Fiercest Dinosaur.* Mankato, Minn.: Bancroft-Sage Publications, 1988.

Sattler, Helen R. *Tyrannosaurus Rex and its Kin: The Mesozoic Monsters.* New York: Lothrop, Lee & Shepard Books, 1989.

___. *The Solar-Powered Dinosaurs.* New York: Lothrop, Lee & Shepard Books, 1992.

Steffof, Rebecca. *Extinction.* New York: Chelsea House Publishers, 1992.

Wallace, Joseph E. *The Audubon Society Pocket Guide to Dinosaurs.* New York: Knopf, 1993.

Some Useful Addresses

The Academy of Natural Sciences
19th Street and The Parkway
Philadelphia, PA 19103

The American Museum of Natural History
Central Park West at 79th Street
New York, NY 10024-5192

Dinosaur National Monument
P.O. Box 210
Dinosaur, CO 81610

Field Museum of Natural History
Roosevelt Road at Lake Shore Drive
Chicago, IL 60605-2496

Museum of the Rockies
South Sixth Street and Kagy Boulevard
Bozeman, MT 59717-0040

National Museum of Natural History
Smithsonian Institution
Tenth Street and Constitution Avenue N.W.
Washington, DC 20002

Natural History Museum of Los Angeles County
900 Exposition Boulevard
Los Angeles, CA 90007

The Peabody Museum
170 Whitney Avenue
New Haven, CT 06511

Royal Ontario Museum
100 Queen's Park
Toronto, Ontario M5S 2C6
Canada

Royal Museum of Paleontology
Box 7500
Drumheller, Alberta T0J 0Y0
Canada

Where to View Dinosaur Tracks

Dinosaur Ridge

This is a national landmark near Morrison, west of Denver, Colorado. The hiking trail allows visitors to stroll along a trackbed from the Cretaceous period.

Dinosaur Valley State Park

This park is in Glen Rose, southwest of Fort Worth, Texas. Part of an original dinosaur trackway was excavated here. It is on view at the American Museum of Natural History in New York City.

Dinosaur State Park

Visitors to this park, in Rocky Hill, south of Hartford, Connecticut, can make plaster casts of dinosaur tracks.

For more information on dinosaur events and sites, write to:

Dinosaur Society
200 Carleton Avenue
East Islip, NY 11730
(516) 277-7855

This organization promotes research and education in the study of dinosaurs. It also publishes *Dino Times*, a monthly magazine for children. Subscriptions are $19.95 a year. *Dinosaur Report*, a quarterly magazine, costs $25 a year.

Photo credits: James P. Rowan: p. 4; Linda J. Moore: pp. 6, 19, 20; Collin Orthner: pp. 11, 30; Denver Museum of Natural History: pp. 15, 16; Bruce Selyem, Museum of the Rockies: p. 38.

Index

48